Learn & Color Nature Series

Reptiles

Ball Python

Learn and Color Nature Series – Reptiles
© 2022 Master Design Marketing, LLC

ISBN: 978-1-947482-33-3

Learn & Color Books
an imprint of Master Design Marketing, LLC
789 State Route 94 E
Fulton, KY 42041
www.LearnAndColor.com

For information about special discounts available for bulk purchases, sales promotions, fund-raising and educational needs, contact Learn & Color Books Company Sales at sales@LearnAndColor.com.

Text prepared by Rose E. A. Carman

Cover and interior design by Faithe F. Thomas
Cover background copyright: Andrea Obzerova / 123RF Stock Photo

Most of the coloring pages are provided by Yulia Znayduk: http://www.supercoloring.com/creators/yulia-znayduk
Most color images provided by DepositPhotos.com

Look for the Scottish Flag somewhere in each of our books.

Sample Pages from
Learn and Color Nature Series – Reptiles

Boa Constrictor
Boa Constrictor

Description

The boa constrictor is a large snake, although it is only modestly sized in comparison to other large snakes, such as the reticulated python, Burmese python, or the occasionally sympatric green anaconda, and can reach lengths from 3 to 13 ft (0.91 to 3.96 m) depending on the locality and the availability of suitable prey. Clear sexual dimorphism is seen in the species, with females generally being larger in both length and girth than males. The usual size of mature female boas is between 7 and 10 ft (2.1 and 3.0 m) whereas males are between 6 and 8 ft (1.8 and 2.4 m). Females commonly exceed 10 ft (3.0 m), particularly in captivity, where lengths up to 12 ft (3.7 m) or even 14 ft (4.3 m) can be seen.

The boa constrictor is a heavy-bodied snake, and large specimens can weigh up to 60 lb (27 kg). Females, the larger sex, more commonly weigh 22 to 33 lb (10 to 15 kg).

The coloring of boa constrictors can vary greatly depending on the locality. However, they are generally a brown, gray, or cream base color, patterned with brown or reddish-brown "saddles" that become more pronounced towards the tail. This coloring gives B. constrictor species the common name of "red-tailed boas." The coloring works as a very effective camouflage in the jungles and forests of its natural range.

Region/Habitat

Boa constrictors can be found through South America north of 35°S, and many other islands along the coasts of South America. An introduced population exists in extreme southern Florida.

They flourish in a wide variety of environmental conditions, from tropical rainforests to arid semidesert country. However, they prefer to live in rainforests due to the humidity and temperature, natural cover from predators, and vast amount of potential prey. They are commonly found in or along rivers and streams.

Diet

The bulk of their diet consists of rodents, but larger lizards and mammals as big as monkeys and wild pigs are also options. Young boa constrictors eat small mice, birds, bats, lizards, and amphibians. The size of the prey item increases as they get older and larger.

It takes the snake about 4–6 days to fully digest the food, depending on the size of the prey and the local temperature. After this, the snake may not eat for a week to several months.

Reproduction

Boa constrictors are viviparous, giving birth to live young. They generally breed in the dry season—between April and August—and are polygynous; thus, males may mate with multiple females. Half of all females breed in a given year, and a larger percentage of males actively attempt to locate a mate. Due to their polygynous nature, many of these males will be unsuccessful.

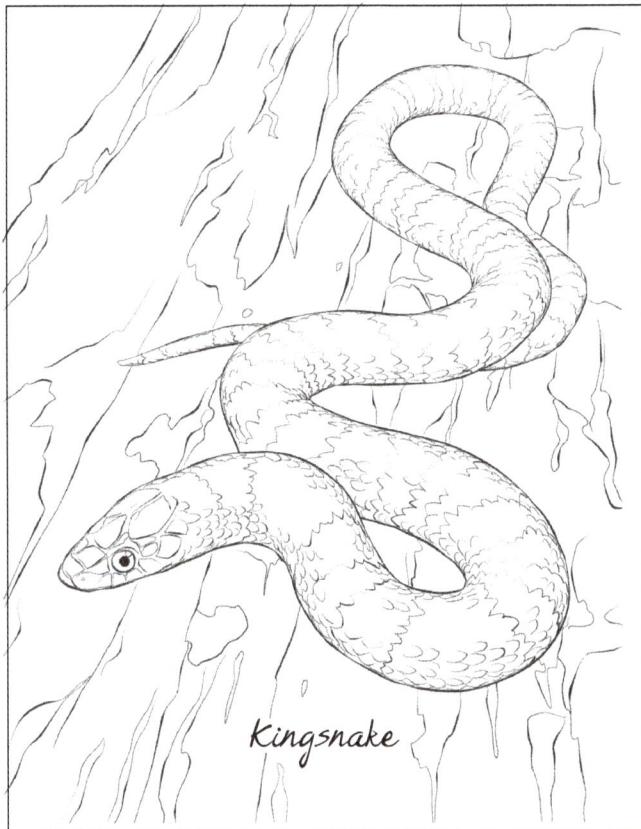

PET ✓

Boa Constrictor

Kingsnake
Lampropeltis

Description

Kingsnakes are colubrid New World members of the genus Lampropeltis, which includes milk snakes and four other species. Among these, about 45 subspecies are recognized. They are nonvenomous.

Kingsnakes vary widely in size and coloration. They can be as small as 24" or as long as 60". Some kingsnakes are colored in muted browns to black, while others are brightly marked in white, reds, yellows, grays, and lavenders that form rings, longitudinal stripes, speckles, and saddle-shaped bands.

Some species, such as the scarlet kingsnake, have coloration and patterning that can cause them to be confused with the highly venomous coral snakes. One of the rhymes to help people distinguish between coral snakes and their nonvenomous lookalikes in the United States is "Red on black, a friend of Jack; red on yellow, kill a fellow."

The kingsnake is one of the most popular pet reptiles due to its ease of care, attractive appearance, and docile demeanor. Due to natural color and pattern variability, snake enthusiasts have selectively bred for a variety of color patterns known as "morphs."

Habitat

Kingsnakes are native to North America, where they are found all over the United States and into Mexico. This genus has adapted to a wide variety of habitats, including tropical forests, shrublands, and deserts.

Kingsnakes are often preyed upon by large vertebrates, such as birds of prey.

Kingsnakes are primarily terrestrial, but they are also known to be capable climbers and swimmers.

Diet

Kingsnakes use constriction to kill their prey and tend to be opportunistic in their diet; they eat other snakes, including venomous snakes. Kingsnakes also eat lizards, rodents, birds, and eggs. The kingsnake is known to be immune to the venom of other snakes and does eat rattlesnakes, but it is not necessarily immune to the venom of snakes from different localities.

Reproduction

The California kingsnake lays eggs, as opposed to giving live birth like some other snakes. Eggs are laid between May and August, which is generally 42–63 days after mating, in preparation the female will have chosen a suitable location. The typical clutch size is five to 12 eggs with an average of nine, though clutches of 20 or more eggs are known. The hatchlings usually emerge another 40–65 days later and are approximately eight to 13 inches in length.

PET ✓

Kingsnake

Alligator

Alligator

Description

An average adult American alligator's weight and length is 790 lbs (360 kg) and 13 ft (4 m), but they sometimes grow to 14 ft (4.4 m) long and weigh over 990 lbs (450 kg). The Chinese alligator is smaller, rarely exceeding 7 ft (2.1 m) in length. Additionally, it weighs considerably less, with males rarely over 100 lbs (45 kg).

The two kinds of white alligators are albino and leucistic. These alligators are practically impossible to find in the wild. They could survive only in captivity and are few in number. The Aquarium of the Americas in New Orleans has leucistic alligators found in a Louisiana swamp in 1987.

Alligators are raised commercially for their meat and their skin, which when tanned is used for the manufacture of luggage, handbags, shoes, belts, and other leather items. Alligator meat is also consumed by humans.

Adult alligators are black or dark olive-brown with white undersides, while juveniles have bright yellow or whitish stripes which sharply contrast against their dark hides, providing them additional camouflage amongst reeds and wetland grasses.

Region/Habitat

Alligators are native to only the United States, Mexico, and China.

American alligators are found in the southeast United States. American alligators live in freshwater environments, such as ponds, marshes, wetlands, rivers, lakes, and swamps, as well as in brackish water.

The Chinese alligator currently is found in only the Yangtze River valley and parts of adjacent provinces and is extremely endangered, with only a few believed to be left in the wild.

Diet

The type of food eaten by alligators depends upon their age and size. When young, alligators eat fish, insects, snails, crustaceans, and worms. As they mature, progressively larger prey is taken, including larger fish such as gar, turtles, and various mammals, as well as birds, deer, and other reptiles. Alligators, unlike the large crocodiles, do not immediately regard a human upon encounter as prey, but may still attack in self-defense if provoked.

Reproduction

The mating season is in late spring. In summer, the female builds a nest of vegetation where the decomposition of the vegetation provides the heat needed to incubate the eggs. The sex of the offspring is determined by the temperature in the nest and is fixed within seven to 21 days.

PET X

Alligator

Ball Python

Ball Python

Python regius

Description

The ball python, also called the royal python, is a python species native to West and Central Africa, where it lives in grasslands, shrublands, and open forests. This nonvenomous constrictor is the smallest of the African pythons, growing to a maximum length of 72 in (182 cm). The name "ball python" refers to its tendency to curl into a ball when stressed or frightened.

The ball python is black or dark brown with light brown blotches on the back and sides. Its white or cream belly is scattered with black markings. It is a stocky snake with a relatively small head and smooth scales. Males typically measure eight to ten subcaudal scales, and females typically measure two to four subcaudal scales. Males are smaller than females. Ball pythons have a maximum weight of 3 lb 9.7 oz (1.635 kg).

Ball pythons are the most popular pet snake and the second most popular pet reptile after the bearded dragon.

Region/Habitat

The ball python is native to west Sub Saharan Africa from Senegal, Mali, Guinea-Bissau, Guinea, Sierra Leone, Liberia, Ivory Coast, Ghana, Benin, and Nigeria through Cameroon, Chad, and the Central African Republic to Sudan and Uganda. It prefers grasslands, savannas, and sparsely wooded areas.

Diet

The diet of the ball python in the wild consists mostly of small mammals and birds. Young ball pythons of less than 28 in (70 cm) prey foremost on small birds. Ball pythons longer than 39 in (100 cm) prey foremost on small mammals. Males prey more frequently on birds, and females more frequently on mammals. Rodents make up a large percentage of the diet; Gambian pouched rats, black rats, rufous-nosed rats, shaggy rats, and striped grass mice are among the species consumed.

Reproduction

Females are oviparous and lay 3-11 rather large, leathery eggs. The eggs hatch after 55 to 60 days. Young male pythons reach sexual maturity at 11–18 months, and females at 20–36 months. Age is only one factor in determining sexual maturity and the ability to breed; weight is the second factor. Males breed at 21 oz (600 g) or more, but in captivity are often not bred until they are 28 oz (800 g). In captivity, breeders generally wait until females are no less than 53 oz (1,500 g). Parental care of the eggs ends once they hatch, and the female leaves the offspring to fend for themselves.

PET ✓

Boa Constrictor

Boa Constrictor

Description

The boa constrictor is a large snake, although it is only modestly sized in comparison to other large snakes, such as the reticulated python, Burmese python, or the occasionally sympatric green anaconda, and can reach lengths from 3 to 13 ft (0.91 to 3.96 m) depending on the locality and the availability of suitable prey. Clear sexual dimorphism is seen in the species, with females generally being larger in both length and girth than males. The usual size of mature female boas is between 7 and 10 ft (2.1 and 3.0 m) whereas males are between 6 and 8 ft (1.8 and 2.4 m). Females commonly exceed 10 ft (3.0 m), particularly in captivity, where lengths up to 12 ft (3.7 m) or even 14 ft (4.3 m) can be seen.

The boa constrictor is a heavy-bodied snake, and large specimens can weigh up to 60 lb (27 kg). Females, the larger sex, more commonly weigh 22 to 33 lb (10 to 15 kg).

The coloring of boa constrictors can vary greatly depending on the locality. However, they are generally a brown, gray, or cream base color, patterned with brown or reddish-brown "saddles" that become more pronounced towards the tail. This coloring gives B. constrictor species the common name of "red-tailed boas." The coloring works as a very effective camouflage in the jungles and forests of its natural range.

Region/Habitat

Boa constrictors can be found through South America north of 35°S, and many other islands along the coasts of South America. An introduced population exists in extreme southern Florida.

They flourish in a wide variety of environmental conditions, from tropical rainforests to arid semidesert country. However, they prefer to live in rainforests due to the humidity and temperature, natural cover from predators, and vast amount of potential prey. They are commonly found in or along rivers and streams.

Diet

The bulk of their diet consists of rodents, but larger lizards and mammals as big as monkeys and wild pigs are also options. Young boa constrictors eat small mice, birds, bats, lizards, and amphibians. The size of the prey item increases as they get older and larger.

It takes the snake about 4–6 days to fully digest the food, depending on the size of the prey and the local temperature. After this, the snake may not eat for a week to several months.

Reproduction

Boa constrictors are viviparous, giving birth to live young. They generally breed in the dry season—between April and August—and are polygynous; thus, males may mate with multiple females. Half of all females breed in a given year, and a larger percentage of males actively attempt to locate a mate. Due to their polygynous nature, many of these males will be unsuccessful.

PET ✓

Boa Constrictor

Bearded Dragon

Bearded Dragon

Pogona

Description

The genus Pogona is in the subfamily Amphibolurinae of the lizard family Agamidae. Bearded dragons are characterized by their broad, triangular heads, flattened bodies, and rows and clusters of spiny scales covering their entire bodies. When threatened, bearded dragons will puff up their bodies and beards to ward off predators and make their somewhat dull spikes more dangerous. Bearded dragons display a hand-waving gesture to show submission, and a head-bobbing display to show dominance between dragons. Some have the ability to slightly change colour during rivalry challenges between males, in response to ambient temperature changes such as turning black to absorb heat, and other stimuli. Males grow up to 24 in (60 cm) long, and females up to 20 in (51 cm).

Introduced into the U.S. as pets during the 1990s, bearded dragons are a species that have gained much popularity as an exotic pet. This popularity has been sustained, even after Australia banned the sale of its wildlife as pets in the 1960s.

Region/Habitat

Bearded dragons originate from deserts and other dry areas in Australia. They live in the arid and subtropical woodlands, scrublands, savannas, shore areas, and into the great interior deserts. They are considered to be semi-arboreal and will quite readily climb and bask at height. They can be found on fallen trees, rocky outcrops, and bushes when basking.

Diet

In the wild, their diet consists primarily of insects, vegetation, and occasionally small rodents.

In captivity, crickets and dubia roaches are the most popular insects fed to bearded dragons, but they can also be fed other insects such as black soldier fly larvae, spiders, locusts, superworms, silkworms, butterworms, fruit flies, grasshoppers, mealworms and hornworms.

Reproduction

When brumation comes to an end the male bearded dragon goes out to find a mate. A courtship ritual occurs where the male starts bobbing his head, waving his arms, and stomping his feet in front of the female.

Through selective breeding, there are many different versions of the Central Inland Bearded Dragon; these are referred to as "morphs." Over the years, many different breeders have selectively bred certain lines to emphasize these traits and will often name their own such as "Dunner," "Sandfire," or "Fire & Ice," all with either their own coloration, patterns, or physical traits.

PET ✓

Chameleon

Chamaeleonidae

Description

Chameleons are a distinctive and highly specialized clade of Old World lizards with 202 species described as of June 2015. This family is most known for their distinct range of colors as they are able to shift in different hues and brightness. Because of the large number of species in their family, there is a large variability in their ability to change color. For some, it is more of a shift of brightness (shades of brown) whereas in others it is a plethora of combinations of colors (reds, yellows, greens, and blues).

Chameleons are distinguished by their zygodactylous feet, their prehensile tail, their laterally compressed bodies, their head casques, their projectile tongues, their swaying gait, and crests or horns on their brow and snout. Chameleons' eyes are independently mobile, and because of this there are two separate, individual images that the brain is analyzing of the chameleon's environment. When hunting prey, they focus forward in coordination, affording the animal stereoscopic vision. The eyes are able to move laterally 180° and vertically 160°.

Chameleons are adapted for climbing and visual hunting. The use of their prehensile tails offers stability when they are moving or resting while on a branch in the canopy; it is often referred to as a "fifth limb." Another character that is helpful for being arboreal is how laterally compressed their bodies are; it is important for them to distribute their weight as evenly as possible on twigs and branches in the trees.

Region/Habitat

Chameleons primarily live in the mainland of sub-Saharan Africa and on the island of Madagascar, although a few species live in other places. There are introduced, feral populations of chameleons in Hawaii, and isolated pockets of feral chameleons have been reported in California, Florida, and Texas.

Chameleons inhabit all kinds of tropical and mountain rain forests, savannas, and sometimes deserts and steppes.

Diet

All chameleons are primarily insectivores that feed by ballistically projecting their long tongues from their mouths to capture prey located some distance away. While the chameleons' tongues are typically thought to be one and a half to two times the length of their bodies (their length excluding the tail), smaller chameleons have recently been found to have proportionately larger tongue apparatuses than their larger counterparts.

Reproduction

The oviparous species lay eggs 3-6 weeks after copulation. The female will dig a hole and deposit her eggs. Clutch sizes vary from two up to 200 eggs. Eggs generally hatch after 4-12 months, depending on the species. Chameleons lay flexible-shelled eggs which are affected by environmental characteristics during incubation.

PET ✅

Chameleon

Copperhead

Copperhead

Agkistrodon contortrix

Description

The eastern copperhead is a species of venomous snake, a pit viper, endemic to eastern North America. It has distinctive, dark brown, hourglass-shaped markings, overlayed on a light reddish brown or brown/gray background. The body type is heavy, rather than slender. Neonates are born with green or yellow tail tips, which progress to a darker brown or black within one year. Copperheads reach an adult length of approximately 3 feet long.

In most of North America, it favors deciduous forest and mixed woodlands. It may occupy rock outcroppings and ledges, but is also found in low-lying, swampy regions. During the winter, it hibernates in dens or limestone crevices, often together with timber rattlesnakes and black rat snakes. The copperhead is known to feed on a wide variety of prey, including invertebrates and vertebrates. Like most pit vipers, the eastern copperhead is generally an ambush predator; it takes up a promising position and waits for suitable prey to arrive. Bites to humans occur due to people unknowingly stepping on them.

Region/Habitat

Eastern copperheads are found in Alabama, Arkansas, Connecticut, Delaware, Florida, Georgia, Illinois, Indiana, Iowa, Kansas, Kentucky, Louisiana, Maryland, Massachusetts, Mississippi, Missouri, Nebraska, New Jersey, New York, North Carolina, Ohio, Oklahoma, Pennsylvania, South Carolina, Tennessee, Texas, Virginia, and West Virginia. In Mexico, it occurs in Chihuahua and Coahuila.

Diet

The eastern copperhead is a diet generalist and is known to feed on a wide variety of prey, including invertebrates and vertebrates. A generalized ontogenetic shift in the diet occurs, with juveniles feeding on higher percentages of invertebrates and ectotherms, and adults feeding on a higher percentage vertebrate endotherms. Both juveniles and adults, though, feed on invertebrates and vertebrates opportunistically. The diet is also known to vary among geographic populations.

Reproduction

Eastern copperheads breed in late summer, but not every year; sometimes, females produce young for several years running, then do not breed at all for a time. They give birth to live young, each of which is about 20 cm (8 in) in total length. The typical litter size is four to seven, but as few as one, or as many as 20 may be seen. Their size apart, the young are similar to the adults, but lighter in color, and with a yellowish-green-marked tip to the tail, which is used to lure lizards and frogs.

PET X

Corn Snake

Pantherophis guttatus

Description

The corn snake is a North American species of rat snake that subdues its small prey by constriction. It is found throughout the southeastern and central United States. Though superficially resembling the venomous copperhead and often killed as a result of this mistaken identity, corn snakes lack functional venom and are harmless. Corn snakes are beneficial to humans by helping to control populations of wild rodent pests that damage crops and spread disease. The corn snake is named for the species' regular presence near grain stores, where it preys on mice and rats that eat harvested corn (maize).

Adult corn snakes have a body length of 2.00–5.97 ft (61–182 cm). In the wild, they usually live around six to eight years, but in captivity can live to an age of 23 years or more. The record for the oldest corn snake in captivity was 32 years and 3 months. They can be distinguished from copperheads by their brighter colors, slender build, round pupils, and lack of heat-sensing pits.

Region/Habitat

Wild corn snakes prefer habitats such as overgrown fields, forest openings, trees, palmetto flatwoods, and abandoned or seldom-used buildings and farms, from sea level to as high as 6,000 feet. Typically, these snakes remain on the ground until the age of four months but can ascend trees, cliffs, and other elevated surfaces. They can be found in the Southeastern United States ranging from New Jersey to the Florida Keys.

In colder regions, snakes brumate during winter. However, in the more temperate climate along the coast, they shelter in rock crevices and logs during cold weather; they also can find shelter in small, closed spaces, such as under a house, and come out on warm days to soak up the heat of the sun.

Diet

Like all snakes, corn snakes are carnivorous and, in the wild, they eat every few days. While most corn snakes eat small rodents, such as the white-footed mouse, they may also eat other reptiles, or amphibians, or climb trees to find unguarded bird eggs.

Reproduction

Corn snakes are relatively easy to breed. They usually breed shortly after the winter cooling. The male courts the female primarily with tactile and chemical cues. If the female is ovulating, the eggs will be fertilized and she will begin sequestering nutrients into the eggs, then secreting a shell.

Egg-laying occurs slightly more than a month after mating, with 12–24 eggs deposited into a warm, moist, hidden location. Once laid, the adult snake abandons the eggs and does not return to them.

PET ✓

Corn Snake

Cottonmouth

Cottonmouth

Agkistrodon piscivorus

Description

Adult cottonmouths commonly exceed 31 in (80 cm) in total length; females are typically smaller than males. The broad head is distinct from the neck, and the snout is blunt in profile with the rim of the top of the head extending forwards slightly further than the mouth. Though the majority of specimens are almost or even totally black (with the exception of the head and facial markings), the color pattern may consist of a brown, gray, tan, yellowish-olive, or blackish ground color, which is overlaid with a series of 10–17 dark brown to almost black crossbands.

Common names include water moccasin, swamp moccasin, black moccasin, and simply viper.

This species is often confused with the copperhead. This is especially true for juveniles, but differences exist. The cottonmouth has broad, dark stripes on the sides of its head that extend back from the eye, whereas the copperhead has only a thin, dark line that divides the pale supralabials from the somewhat darker color of the head.

Region/Habitat

The cottonmouth is one of the world's few semiaquatic vipers, and is native to the southeastern United States. As an adult, it is large and capable of delivering a painful and potentially fatal bite. When threatened, it may respond by coiling its body and displaying its fangs. Individuals may bite when feeling threatened or being handled in any way. It is found in or near water, particularly in slow-moving and shallow lakes, streams, and marshes. It is a capable swimmer and is known to occasionally enter bays and estuaries and swim between barrier islands and the mainland.

Diet

Its diet includes mammals, birds, amphibians, fish, snakes, small turtles, and small alligators. Cannibalism has also been reported. Normally, though, the bulk of its diet consists of fish and frogs. On occasion, juvenile specimens feed on invertebrates. Catfish are often eaten, although the sharp spines sometimes cause injuries.

Reproduction

Agkistrodon piscivorus is ovoviviparous, with females usually giving birth to one to 16 live young and possibly as many as 20. Litters of six to eight are the most common. Neonates are 22–35 cm in length. If weather conditions are favorable and food is readily available, growth is rapid and females may reproduce at less than three years of age and a total length of as little as 60 cm. The young are born in August or September, while mating may occur during any of the warmer months of the year, at least in certain parts of its range.

PET ✗

Crocodile
Crocodylus acutus

Description

The American crocodile is a species of crocodilian found in the Neotropics. It is the most widespread of the four extant species of crocodiles from the Americas, with populations present from South Florida and the coasts of Mexico to as far south as Peru and Venezuela.

The American crocodile is one of the largest crocodile species. Males can reach lengths of 20 ft, weighing up to 2,000 pounds. Like all true crocodilians, the American crocodile is a quadruped, with four short, stocky legs; a long, powerful tail; and a scaly hide with rows of ossified scutes running down its back and tail. Its snout is elongated and includes a strong pair of jaws. Its eyes have nictitating membranes for protection, along with lacrimal glands, which produce tears.

The nostrils, eyes, and ears are situated on the top of its head, so the rest of the body can be concealed underwater for surprise attacks. Camouflage also helps it prey on food. The snout is longer and narrower than that of the American alligator. American crocodiles are also paler and more grayish than the relatively dark-hued American alligator. This crocodile species normally crawls on its belly, but it can also "high walk."

Adults have a uniform grayish-green coloration with white or yellow undersides, while juveniles have dark cross-banding on the tail and back.

Region/Habitat

The habitat of the American crocodile consists largely of coastal areas. It is also found in river systems, but tends to prefer salinity, resulting in the species congregating in brackish lakes, mangrove swamps, lagoons, cays, and small islands. The American crocodile is the only species other than the saltwater crocodile to commonly live and thrive in saltwater. They can be found on beaches and small island formations without any freshwater source, such as many cays and islets across the Caribbean.

Diet

In Florida, bass, tarpon, and mullet, large crabs, snakes, mammals that habit the coastal regions of the Everglades, such as opossums and raccoons appeared to be the primary prey of American crocodiles. In Haiti, adults appeared to live largely off of various birds, including herons, storks, flamingos, pelicans, grebes, coots, and moorhens, followed by concentrations of marine fish including tilapia and cichlasoma, at times being seen to capture turtles, dogs, and goats.

Reproduction

American crocodiles breed in late fall or early winter. In February or March, gravid females will begin to create nests of sand, mud, and dead vegetation along the water's edge. About one month later, when it is time to lay, the female will dig a wide hole diagonally into the side of the nest and lay 30 to 70 eggs in it.

PET ✗

Crocodile

Dragon

Dragon

A dragon is a reptile-like legendary creature that appears in the folklore of many cultures worldwide. Beliefs about dragons vary considerably through regions, but dragons in western cultures since the High Middle Ages have often been depicted as winged, horned, four-legged, and capable of breathing fire. Dragons in eastern cultures are usually depicted as wingless, four-legged, serpentine creatures with above-average intelligence. Commonalities between dragons' traits are often a hybridization of feline, avian, and reptilian features. Scholars believe huge extinct or migrating crocodiles bear the closest resemblance, especially when encountered in forested or swampy areas, and are most likely the template of modern Oriental dragon imagery.

Draconic creatures are first described in the mythologies of the ancient Near East and appear in ancient Mesopotamian art and literature. Stories about storm-gods slaying giant serpents occur throughout nearly all Indo-European and Near Eastern mythologies. Famous prototypical draconic creatures include the mušhuššu of ancient Mesopotamia; Apep in Egyptian mythology; Vrtra in the Rigveda; the Leviathan in the Hebrew Bible; Grand'Goule in the Poitou region in France; Python, Ladon, Wyvern, Kulshedra in Albanian mythology; and the Lernaean Hydra in Greek mythology; Jörmungandr, Níðhöggr, and Fafnir in Norse mythology; and the dragon from Beowulf.

The word dragon entered the English language in the early 13th century from Old French dragon, which in turn comes from Latin: draconem (nominative draco) meaning "huge serpent, dragon," from Ancient Greek δράκων, "serpent, giant seafish." The Greek and Latin term referred to any great serpent, not necessarily mythological. The Greek word δράκων is most likely derived from the Greek verb δέρκομαι (dérkomai) meaning "I see." This is thought to have referred to something with a "deadly glance," or unusually bright or "sharp" eyes, or because a snake's eyes appear to be always open; each eye actually sees through a big transparent scale in its eyelids, which are permanently shut. The Greek word probably derives from an Indo-European base derk- meaning "to see"; the Sanskrit root दृश् (dṛś-) also means "to see."

Eastern Green Mamba

Dendroaspis angusticeps

Description

The eastern green mamba is a highly venomous snake species of the mamba genus Dendroaspis native to the coastal regions of southern East Africa. It has a slender build with a bright green back and green-yellow ventral scales. Adult females average around 6 ft 7 in in length, and males are smaller.

A shy and elusive species, the eastern green mamba is rarely seen. This elusiveness is usually attributed to its arboreal habitat and green colouration, which acts as camouflage in its natural environment. It has also been observed to use ambush predation, like many vipers, contrary to the active foraging style typical of other elapid snakes. It preys on birds, eggs, bats, and rodents such as mice, rats, and gerbils.

Its venom consists of both neurotoxins and cardiotoxins. Symptoms of envenomation include swelling of the injection site, dizziness, and nausea, accompanied by difficulty breathing and swallowing, irregular heartbeat, and convulsions progressing to respiratory paralysis. Bites that result in severe envenomation can quickly be fatal.

Region/Habitat

The eastern green mamba is native to regions near the coastlines of Southern Africa and East Africa. An elusive species, it is primarily arboreal (living in trees) and usually well camouflaged in foliage. Some herpetologists believe its habitat is limited to tropical rainforests in coastal lowlands. Other experts believe it can also be found in coastal bush, and dune and montane forest. Unlike its close relative the black mamba, the eastern green mamba is rarely found in open terrain and prefers relatively dense, well-shaded vegetation. As well as wild forest habitats, it is also commonly found in thickets and farm trees such as citrus, mango, coconut, and cashew. In coastal East Africa, it is known to enter houses and may even shelter in thatched-roof dwellings.

Diet

The eastern green mamba preys primarily on birds and their eggs, and small mammals including bats. It is also believed to eat arboreal lizards. It uses a sit-and-wait strategy. The species is also known to raid the nests of young birds.

Reproduction

The eastern green mamba is solitary except during breeding season. Males locate females by following a scent trail. The male courts the female by aligning his body along the female's while rapidly tongue-flicking. Courtship and mating take place in trees, after which the female can lay 4–17 eggs (10–15 on average), occurring in October and November. The eggs are small and elongated, and usually laid in leaf litter in hollow trees. The incubation period is around three months. When the young emerge, they are approximately 12 to 18 in in the wild, and 17 in in captivity.

PET ✗

Eastern Green Mamba

Galápagos Tortoise

Galápagos Tortoise

Chelonoidis niger

Description

Galápagos tortoises are native to seven of the Galápagos Islands. Shell size and shape vary between subspecies and populations. On islands with humid highlands, the tortoises are larger, with domed shells and short necks; on islands with dry lowlands, the tortoises are smaller, with "saddleback" shells and long necks. Tortoise numbers declined from over 250,000 in the 16th century to a low of around 15,000 in the 1970s. This decline was caused by overexploitation of the subspecies.

The tortoises have a large bony shell of a dull brown or grey color. The plates of the shell are fused with the ribs in a rigid protective structure that is integral to the skeleton. Lichens can grow on the shells of these slow-moving animals. Tortoises keep a characteristic scute (shell segment) pattern on their shells throughout life, though the annual growth bands are not useful for determining age because the outer layers are worn off with time. A tortoise can withdraw its head, neck, and forelimbs into its shell for protection.

Behavior

The tortoises are ectothermic (cold-blooded), so they bask for 1–2 hours after dawn to absorb the sun's heat through their dark shells before actively foraging for 8–9 hours a day. They travel mostly in the early morning or late afternoon between resting and grazing areas. Tortoises sometimes rest in mud wallows or rain-formed pools, which may be both a thermoregulatory response during cool nights, and a protection from parasites.

Diet

The tortoises are herbivores that consume a diet of cacti, grasses, leaves, lichens, berries, melons, oranges, and milkweed. They acquire most of their moisture from the dew and sap in vegetation (particularly the Opuntia cactus); therefore, they can survive longer than 6 months without water. They can endure up to a year when deprived of all food and water, surviving by breaking down their body fat to produce water as a byproduct.

Reproduction

Females journey up to several miles in July to November to reach nesting areas of dry, sandy coast. Nest digging is a tiring and elaborate task which may take the female several hours a day over many days to complete. It is carried out blindly using only the hind legs to dig a cylindrical hole, in which the tortoise then lays up to 16 spherical, hard-shelled eggs. The female makes a muddy plug for the nest hole out of soil mixed with urine, seals the nest by pressing down firmly with her plastron, and leaves them to be incubated by the sun.

PET ✕

Garter Snake

Thamnophis

Description

Garter snake is a common name for generally harmless, small to medium-sized snakes belonging to the genus Thamnophis in the family Colubridae. Native to North and Central America, species in the genus Thamnophis can be found from the subarctic plains of Canada to Costa Rica.

With about 35 recognized species and subspecies, garter snakes are highly variable in appearance. They generally have large round eyes, round pupils, a slender build, keeled scales, and a pattern of longitudinal stripes that may or may not include spots (although some don't have stripes at all). They also vary significantly in total length from as short as 18 to as long as 51 inches.

If disturbed a garter snake may coil and strike but typically it will hide its head and flail its tail. These snakes will also discharge a malodorous, musky-scented secretion from a gland near the cloaca. They often use these techniques to escape when ensnared by a predator. They will also slither into the water to escape a predator on land. Hawks, crows, egrets, herons, cranes, raccoons, otters, and other snake species will eat garter snakes, with even shrews and frogs eating the juveniles.

Being heterothermic, like all reptiles, garter snakes bask in the sun to regulate their body temperature.

Region/Habitat

Garter snakes are present throughout most of North America. Their wide distribution is due to their varied diets and adaptability to different habitats, with varying proximity to water. However in the western part of North America these snakes are more aquatic than in the eastern portion. Garter snakes live in a variety of habitats, including forests, woodlands, fields, grasslands, and lawns, but never far from water, often an adjacent wetland, stream or pond. Garter snakes are often found near small ponds with tall weeds.

Diet

Garter snakes, like all snakes, are carnivorous. Their diet consists of almost any creature they are capable of overpowering: slugs, earthworms (nightcrawlers are toxic to garter snakes), leeches, lizards, amphibians (including frog eggs), minnows, and rodents. When living near water they will eat other aquatic animals. Food is swallowed whole. Garter snakes often adapt to eating whatever they can find because food can be either scarce or abundant.

Reproduction

Garter snakes have complex systems of pheromonal communication. Male snakes giving off both male and female pheromones have been shown to garner more copulations than normal males in the mating balls that form at the den when females enter the mating melee. A snake hatch can include as many as 57 young.

PET ✓

Garter Snake

Gecko

Gecko

Gekkota

Description

Geckos are small, mostly carnivorous lizards that have a wide distribution, found on every continent except Antarctica. Belonging to the infraorder Gekkota, geckos are found in warm climates throughout the world. They range from 0.6 to 23.6 inches. Geckos are the most species-rich group of lizards, with about 1,500 different species worldwide.

All geckos, except species in the family Eublepharidae lack eyelids; instead, the outer surface of the eyeball has a transparent membrane, the cornea. They have a fixed lens within each iris that enlarges in darkness to let in more light. Since they cannot blink, species without eyelids generally lick their own corneas when they need to clear them of dust and dirt, in order to keep them clean and moist.

Unlike most lizards, geckos are usually nocturnal and have excellent night vision; their colour vision in low light is 350 times more sensitive than human eyes.

Habitat

Many species are well known for their specialized toe pads, which enable them to grab and climb onto smooth and vertical surfaces, and even cross indoor ceilings with ease. Geckos are well known to people who live in warm regions of the world, where several species make their home inside human habitations. These, for example the house gecko, become part of the indoor menagerie and are often welcomed. Like most lizards, geckos can lose their tails in defence, a process called autotomy; the predator may attack the wriggling tail, allowing the gecko to escape.

Diet

Leopard geckos are opportunistic predators that eat a variety of prey items. Invertebrates are presumed to make up the majority of wild geckos' diets, but in captivity they will also eat small vertebrate prey if given the opportunity, including baby "pink" mice and even hatchling leopard geckos, though sufficiently fed geckos will not cannibalize young.

Reproduction

Leopard geckos typically breed in the summer. Females can store sperm over the course of their breeding season, and produce up to three clutches from one or two copulations. Females can lay about six to eight clutches of two eggs; eggs are laid approximately 21 to 28 days after mating. The average amount of time it takes for a newborn to hatch is anywhere between 35 and 89 days, although it is usually closer to the latter. Baby geckos will have an "egg tooth," a calcareous tip at the end of its snout to help break their egg shell. Their "egg tooth" will fall off within one to two days. In addition to this, their skin will usually shed within 24 hours of hatching.

PET ✅

Gila Monster

Heloderma suspectum

Description

The Gila monster is a species of venomous lizard native to the Southwestern United States and the northwestern Mexican state of Sonora. It is a heavy, typically slow-moving reptile, up to 2.0 ft long, and is the only venomous lizard native to the United States. The Gila monster is sluggish in nature, so is not generally dangerous and may very rarely pose a real threat to humans. Yet, its exaggeratedly fearsome reputation has led to it sometimes being killed, in spite of being protected by state law in Arizona.

Gila monsters spend 90% of their lifetime underground in burrows or rocky shelters. They are active in the morning during the dry season (spring and early summer). The lizards move to different shelters every 4–5 days up to the beginning of the summer season. By doing so, they optimize for a suitable microhabitat for survival. Later in the summer, they may be active on warm nights or after a thunderstorm. They maintain a surface body temperature of about 86 °F.

Region/Habitat

The Gila monster is found in the Southwestern United States and Mexico, a range including Sonora, Arizona, parts of California, Nevada, Utah, and New Mexico. They inhabit scrubland, succulent desert, and oak woodland, seeking shelter in burrows, thickets, and under rocks in locations with a favorable microclimate and adequate humidity. Gila monsters depend on water resources, and might be observed in puddles of water after a summer rain. They avoid living in open areas, such as flats and open grasslands.

Diet

The Gila monster's diet consists of a variety of food items – small mammals (such as young rabbits, hares, mice, ground squirrels, other rodents, etc.), small birds, snakes, lizards, frogs, insects, carrion, and the eggs of birds, lizards, snakes, and tortoises. Three to four extensive meals in spring are claimed to give them enough energy for a whole season. Nevertheless, they feed whenever they come across suitable prey. Adults may eat up to one-third of their body weight in one meal.

Reproduction

The female lays eggs at the end of May into June. A clutch may consist of up to six (rarely up to eight) eggs. The incubation in captivity lasts about five months, depending on the incubation temperature. The hatchlings are about 6.3 inches long and can bite and inject venom as soon as they are hatched.

The Gila monster hatches near the end of October and immediately proceed into hibernation without surfacing. They then appear on the surface from May through June the following year when prey should be abundant.

PET ✕

Gila Monsters

Hognose Snake

Hognose Snake

Heterodon

Description

Heterodon is a genus of harmless colubrid snakes endemic to North America. They have upturned snouts and are perhaps best known for their characteristic threat displays. Three species are currently recognized. Members of the genus are commonly known as hognose snakes, hog-nosed snakes, North American hog-nosed snakes, and sometimes puff adders (though they should not be confused with the venomous African vipers of the genus Bitis).

Adults grow to 12-47 inches in total length. The body is stout and the head is slightly distinct from the neck. The latter is expandable, the anterior ribs being capable of spreading to flatten that portion of the body, similar to a cobra.

The color pattern is extremely variable. They tend to be sandy-colored with black and white markings, but some species vary from reds, greens, oranges, browns, to black depending on locality. They are sometimes blotched and sometimes solid-colored.

Behavior

When threatened, the hognose snake will flatten its neck and raise its head off the ground, similar to a cobra, and hiss. It may sometimes feign strikes, but is extremely reluctant to bite. This behavior has earned the hognose snake several nicknames, such as "hissing adder." If this threat display does not work, the hognose snake will often roll onto its back and play dead with its mouth open, going as far as to emit a foul musk. If the snake is rolled upright while in this state, it will often roll over again as if to insist that it is really dead.

Unfortunately due to their appearance and impressive defensive display, hognose snakes are commonly mistaken to be copperheads and subsequently killed.

Diet

The bulk of the Heterodon species diet is made up of rodents and lizards. H. platirhinos is an exception, and specializes in feeding on toads, having an immunity to the toxins that toads secrete.

Reproduction

Adult western hognose snakes have been observed in copulation as early as February and March. The species is oviparous, with females laying 4-23 elongate, thin-shelled eggs in June-August. The eggs take approximately 60 days to hatch. Each hatchling is 5-9 inches in total length, and reaches sexual maturity after approximately two years (this is predominantly based on size, not so much age).

PET ✅

Green Iguana
Iguana Iguana

Description

The green iguana, also known as the American iguana or the common green iguana, is a large, arboreal, mostly herbivorous species of lizard of the genus Iguana. Usually, this animal is simply called the iguana. The green iguana ranges over a large geographic area; it is native from southern Brazil and Paraguay as far north as Mexico, and has been introduced from South America to Puerto Rico and is very common throughout the island, where it is colloquially known as gallina de palo ("bamboo chicken" or "chicken of the tree") and considered an invasive species; in the United States, feral populations also exist in South Florida (including the Florida Keys), Hawaii, the U.S. Virgin Islands, and the Rio Grande Valley of Texas. Green iguanas have also successfully colonised the island of Anguilla, arriving on the island in 1995 after rafting across the Caribbean from Guadeloupe, where they were introduced.

A herbivore, it has adapted significantly with regard to locomotion and osmoregulation as a result of its diet. It grows to 4.9 ft in length from head to tail, although a few specimens have grown more than 6.6 ft with bodyweights upward of 20 lbs.

Commonly found in captivity as a pet due to its calm disposition and bright colors, it can be very demanding to care for properly. Space requirements and the need for special lighting and heat can prove challenging to the hobbyist.

Habitat

Green iguanas are diurnal, arboreal, and are often found near water. Agile climbers, iguana can fall up to 50 feet and land unhurt (iguanas use their hind leg claws to clasp leaves and branches to break a fall). During cold, wet weather, green iguanas prefer to stay on the ground for greater warmth. When swimming, iguanas remain submerged, letting their legs hang limply against their sides. They propel through the water with powerful tail strokes.

While they may often be found in trees, these animals are well-known burrowers. They have been observed burrowing in canals, levees, and along seawalls in southern Florida.

Diet

Green iguanas are primarily herbivores, with captives feeding on leaves such as turnip, mustard, and dandelion greens, flowers, fruit, and growing shoots of upwards of 100 different species of plant. In Panama, one of the green iguana's favorite foods is the wild plum (Spondias mombin).

Reproduction

Green iguanas are oviparous, with females laying clutches of 20 to 71 eggs once per year. The female gives no parental protection after egg laying, apart from defending the nesting burrow during excavation. The hatchlings emerge from the nest after 10–15 weeks of incubation.

PET ✅

Green iguana

Kingsnake

Kingsnake

Lampropeltis

Description

Kingsnakes are colubrid New World members of the genus Lampropeltis, which includes milk snakes and four other species. Among these, about 45 subspecies are recognized. They are nonvenomous.

Kingsnakes vary widely in size and coloration. They can be as small as 24" or as long as 60". Some kingsnakes are colored in muted browns to black, while others are brightly marked in white, reds, yellows, grays, and lavenders that form rings, longitudinal stripes, speckles, and saddle-shaped bands.

Some species, such as the scarlet kingsnake, have coloration and patterning that can cause them to be confused with the highly venomous coral snakes. One of the rhymes to help people distinguish between coral snakes and their nonvenomous lookalikes in the United States is "Red on black, a friend of Jack; red on yellow, kill a fellow."

The kingsnake is one of the most popular pet reptiles due to its ease of care, attractive appearance, and docile demeanor. Due to natural color and pattern variability, snake enthusiasts have selectively bred for a variety of color patterns known as "morphs."

Habitat

Kingsnakes are native to North America, where they are found all over the United States and into Mexico. This genus has adapted to a wide variety of habitats, including tropical forests, shrublands, and deserts.

Kingsnakes are often preyed upon by large vertebrates, such as birds of prey.

Kingsnakes are primarily terrestrial, but they are also known to be capable climbers and swimmers.

Diet

Kingsnakes use constriction to kill their prey and tend to be opportunistic in their diet; they eat other snakes, including venomous snakes. Kingsnakes also eat lizards, rodents, birds, and eggs. The kingsnake is known to be immune to the venom of other snakes and does eat rattlesnakes, but it is not necessarily immune to the venom of snakes from different localities.

Reproduction

The California kingsnake lays eggs, as opposed to giving live birth like some other snakes. Eggs are laid between May and August, which is generally 42–63 days after mating; in preparation the female will have chosen a suitable location. The typical clutch size is five to 12 eggs with an average of nine, though clutches of 20 or more eggs are known. The hatchlings usually emerge another 40–65 days later and are approximately eight to 13 inches in length.

PET ✅

King Cobra

Ophiophagus hannah

Description

The king cobra is the world's longest venomous snake, with an average length of 10.4 to 13.1 ft, reaching a maximum of 19.2 ft. Its skin colour varies across the habitats, from black with white stripes to unbroken brownish grey. It preys chiefly on other snakes, including its own species. Unlike other snakes, it rarely hunts other vertebrates, such as rodents and lizards.

Like most cobras and mambas, the king cobra's threat display includes spreading its neck-flap, raising its head upright, puffing, and hissing. Despite its fearsome reputation, the king cobra avoids confrontation with humans whenever possible. When provoked, however, it is capable of striking a target at long range and well above the ground. Rather than biting and retreating, it may sustain its bite and inject a large quantity of venom, which is a medical emergency.

Regarded as the national reptile of India, this species has an eminent position in mythology and folk traditions of India, Sri Lanka, and Myanmar.

Region/Habitat

The king cobra has a wide distribution in South and Southeast Asia. It occurs up to an elevation of 6,600 ft from the Terai in India and southern Nepal to the Brahmaputra River basin in Bhutan and northeast India, Bangladesh, and to Myanmar, southern China, Cambodia, Thailand, Laos, Vietnam, Malaysia, Singapore, Indonesia, and the Philippines.

Diet

The king cobra is an apex predator and dominant over all other snakes except large pythons. Its diet consists primarily of other snakes and lizards, including Indian cobra, banded krait, rat snake, pythons, green whip snake, keelback, banded wolf snake, and Blyth's reticulated snake. It also hunts Malabar pit viper and hump-nosed pit viper by following their odour trails. When food is scarce, it also feeds on other small vertebrates, such as birds, and lizards. In some cases, the cobra constricts its prey using its muscular body, though this is uncommon. After a large meal, it lives for many months without another one because of its slow metabolic rate.

Reproduction

The king cobra is the only snake that builds a nest using dry leaf litter, starting from late March to late May. Most nests are located at the base of trees. They consist of several layers and have mostly one chamber, into which the female lays eggs. Clutch size ranges from seven to 43 eggs. Hatchlings are between 14.8 and 23.0 inches long.

The venom of hatchlings is as potent as that of the adults. They may be brightly marked, but these colours often fade as they mature. They are alert and nervous, being highly aggressive if disturbed. The average lifespan of a wild king cobra is about 20 years.

PET ✗

King Cobra

Rat Snake

Rat Snake
Pantherophis

Description

Rat snakes are members – along with kingsnakes, milk snakes, vine snakes, and indigo snakes – of the subfamily Colubrinae of the family Colubridae. They are medium to large constrictors and are found throughout much of the Northern Hemisphere. They feed primarily on rodents. Many species make attractive and docile pets and one, the corn snake, is one of the most popular reptile pets in the world. As with all snakes, they can be defensive when approached too closely, handled, or restrained, but bites are not serious.

Like nearly all colubrids, rat snakes pose no threat to humans. Rat snakes were long believed to be completely nonvenomous, but recent studies have shown that some Old World species do possess small amounts of venom, though the amount is negligible relative to humans.

Behavior

An agile climber, the rat snake is at home from the ground to the tree tops in many types of hardwood forest and cypress stands, along tree-lined streams and fields, and even around barns and sheds in close proximity to people. Within its range, almost any environment rich in rodents, and vertical escape options, proves a suitable habitat for the rat snake.

When startled, the rat snake stops and remains motionless with its body held in a series of wave-like kinks. The snake will also rattle its tail against whatever it is lying on, making an audible buzzing sound. The rat snake will defend itself by raising its head and bluffing a strike. If handled, it will musk a victim by releasing the foul-smelling contents of its cloaca.

Diet

A scent-hunter and a powerful constrictor, the rat snake feeds primarily on small mammals, birds, and bird eggs. Neonates and juveniles prefer a diet of frogs and lizards.

Reproduction

Breeding in rat snakes takes place from April to July. Females reach sexual maturity at 7–9 years of age. They deposit five to 27 eggs around mid-summer, and the 9.8–11.8 inch hatchlings usually emerge in September.

Rat snakes are available captive-bred in the United States pet trade, and they have been bred for mutations such as leucistic, albino, and scaleless. However, they are not as popular as other colubrids such as corn snakes, kingsnakes, milksnakes, and hognose snakes.

PET ✅

Rattlesnake

Crotalus and Sistrurus

Description

Rattlesnakes are venomous snakes that form the genera Crotalus and Sistrurus of the subfamily Crotalinae (the pit vipers). All rattlesnakes are vipers. Rattlesnakes are predators that live in a wide array of habitats, hunting small animals such as birds and rodents.

Rattlesnakes receive their name from the rattle located at the end of their tails, which makes a loud rattling noise when vibrated that deters predators or serves as a warning to passers-by. Rattlesnakes are the leading contributor to snakebite injuries in North America, but rarely bite unless provoked or threatened. The bites are seldom fatal.

The 36 known species of rattlesnakes have between 65 and 70 subspecies, all native to the Americas, ranging from British Columbia through Ontario in southern Canada, to central Argentina. The largest rattlesnake, the eastern diamondback, can measure up to 8 feet in length.

Rattlesnakes are preyed upon by hawks, weasels, king snakes, and a variety of other species. Rattlesnakes are heavily preyed upon as neonates, while they are still weak and immature. Large numbers of rattlesnakes are killed by humans. Rattlesnake populations in many areas are severely threatened by habitat destruction, poaching, and extermination campaigns.

Habitat

Rattlesnakes are found in almost every habitat type capable of supporting terrestrial ectothermic vertebrates, but individual species can have extremely specific habitat requirements, only able to live within certain plant associations in a narrow range of altitudes. Most species live near open, rocky areas. Rocks offer them cover from predators, plentiful prey (e.g. rodents, lizards, insects, etc. that live amidst the rocks), and open basking areas. However, rattlesnakes can also be found in a wide variety of other habitats, including prairies, marshes, deserts, and forests.

Diet

Rattlesnakes typically consume mice, rats, rabbits, squirrels, small birds, and other small animals. They lie in wait for their prey, or hunt for it in holes. The prey is killed quickly with a venomous bite as opposed to constriction. The prey is then ingested head first, which allows wings and limbs to fold at the joints in a manner that minimizes the girth of the meal.

Reproduction

Most rattlesnake species mate during the summer or fall, while some species mate only in the spring, or during both the spring and fall. Although many kinds of snakes and other reptiles are oviparous (lay eggs), rattlesnakes are ovoviviparous (give birth to live young after carrying eggs inside).

PET ✗

Rattlesnake

Red-Eared Slider

Red-Eared Slider

Trachemys scripta elegans

Description

The red-eared slider or red-eared terrapin (Trachemys scripta elegans) is a subspecies of the pond slider, a semiaquatic turtle belonging to the family Emydidae. It is the most popular pet turtle in the United States. It is the most commonly traded turtle in the world.

The red-eared slider is native to the Southern United States and northern Mexico, but has become established in other places because of pet releases, and has become invasive in many areas where it outcompetes native species. The red-eared slider is included in the list of the world's 100 most invasive species published by the International Union for Conservation of Nature.

The red-eared slider gets its name from the small, red stripe around its ears, or where its ears would be, and from its ability to slide quickly off rocks and logs into the water.

The carapace of this species can reach more than 16 inches in length, but the typical length ranges from 6 to 8 inches. They typically live between 20 and 30 years, although some individuals have lived for more than 40 years. Their life expectancy is shorter when they are kept in captivity. The quality of their living environment has a strong influence on their lifespans.

Region/Habitat

The red-eared slider originated from the area around the Mississippi River and the Gulf of Mexico, in warm climates in the Southeastern United States. Their native areas range from the southeast of Colorado to Virginia and Florida. In nature, they inhabit areas with a source of still, warm water, such as ponds, lakes, swamps, creeks, streams, or slow-flowing rivers, where they are able to leave the water easily by climbing onto rocks or tree trunks so they can warm up in the sun. Individuals are often found sunbathing in a group or even on top of each other.

Diet

The red-eared slider is mostly herbivorous as an adult, but primarily carnivorous as a juvenile. The adults eat algae, fish, tadpoles, crayfish, seeds, plants, aquatic vegetation, insects, worms, and mollusks. This subspecies, like all aquatic turtles, can only swallow food when in the water.

Reproduction

After mating, the female spends extra time basking to keep her eggs warm. She may also have a change of diet, eating only certain foods, or not eating as much as she normally would. A female can lay 2-30 eggs depending on body size. One female can lay up to five clutches in the same year, and clutches are usually spaced 12-36 days apart. Incubation takes 59-112 days. Late-season hatchlings may spend the winter in the nest and emerge when the weather warms in the spring.

PET ✓

Sea Turtle

Chelonioidea

Description

In general, sea turtles have a more fusiform body plan than their terrestrial or freshwater counterparts. This tapering at both ends reduces volume and means that sea turtles cannot retract their head and limbs into their shells for protection, unlike many other turtles and tortoises. However, the streamlined body plan reduces friction and drag in the water and allows sea turtles to swim more easily and swiftly.

The leatherback sea turtle is the largest sea turtle, measuring 6–9 feet in length, 3–5 feet in width, and weighing up to 1,500 pounds. Other sea turtle species are smaller, being mostly 2–4 feet long and proportionally narrower.

Region/Habitat

Sea turtles are generally found in the waters over continental shelves. During the first few years of life, sea turtles spend most of their time in the pelagic zone floating in seaweed mats, in which they find food, shelter, and water. Once the sea turtle has reached adulthood it moves closer to the shore.

Diet

The loggerhead, Kemp's ridley, olive ridley, and hawksbill sea turtles are omnivorous their entire life. They eat a wide variety of plant and animal life including decapods, seagrasses, seaweed, sponges, mollusks, cnidarians, Echinoderms, worms, and fish.

The diet of green sea turtles changes with age. Juveniles are omnivorous, but as they mature they become exclusively herbivorous. Green sea turtles have a serrated jaw that is used to eat sea grass and algae.

Leatherback sea turtles feed almost exclusively on jellyfish and help control jellyfish populations. Hawksbill sea turtles principally eat sponges, which constitute 70–95% of their diets in the Caribbean.

Reproduction

It takes decades for sea turtles to reach sexual maturity. Mature sea turtles may migrate thousands of miles to reach breeding sites. After mating at sea, adult female sea turtles return to land to lay their eggs. The mature nesting female hauls herself onto the beach, nearly always at night, and finds suitable sand in which to create a nest. Using her hind flippers, she digs a circular hole 16 to 20 inches deep. After the hole is dug, the female then starts filling the nest with soft-shelled eggs. A typical clutch may contain 50–350 eggs. After laying, she re-fills the nest with sand, and then camouflages the nest with vegetation until it is relatively undetectable visually. She may also dig decoy nests. The whole process takes 30 to 60 minutes. She then returns to the ocean, leaving the eggs untended.

The eggs incubate for 50–60 days. The baby sea turtles break free of the egg shell, dig through the sand, and crawl into the sea.

PET ✗

Sea Turtle

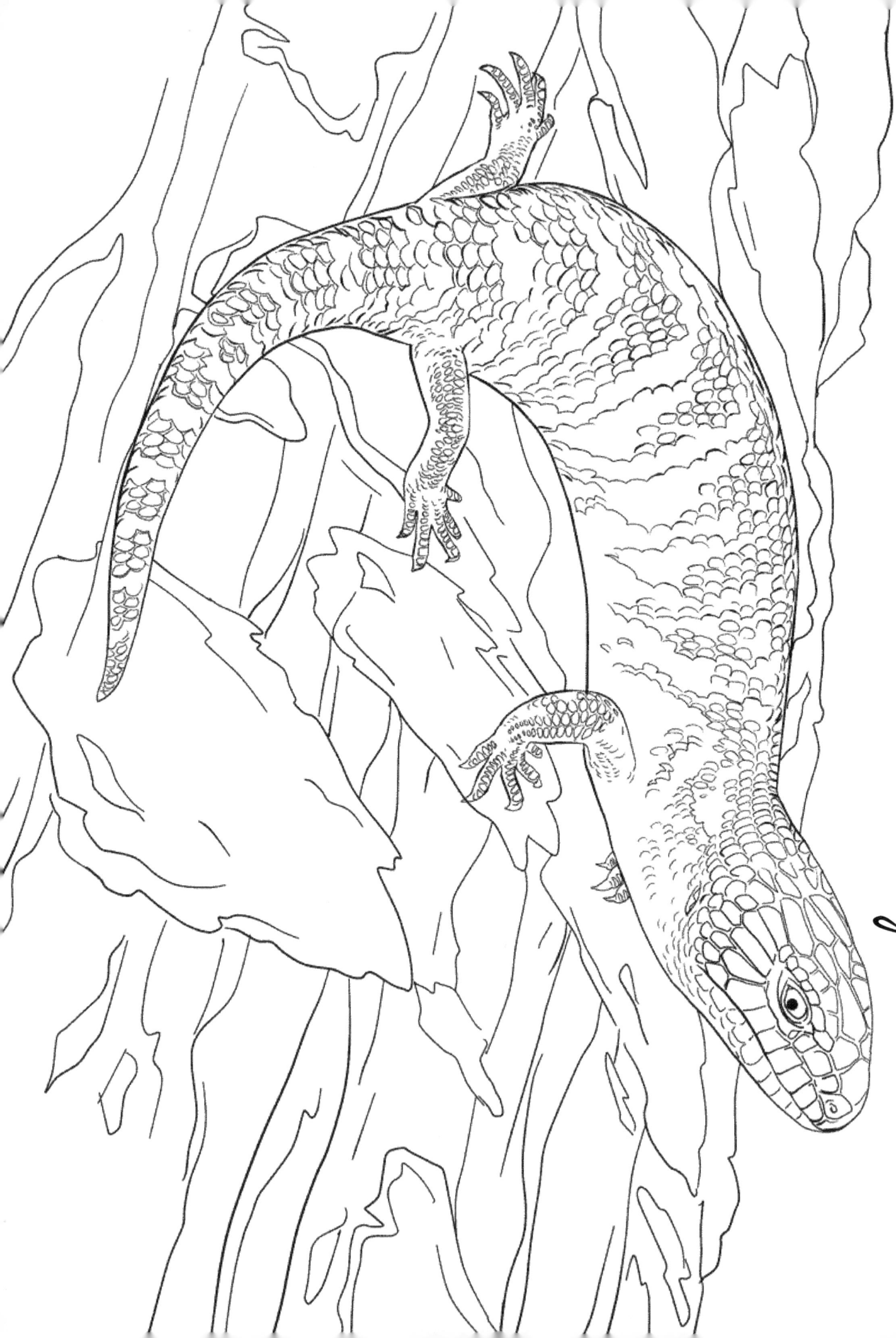

Eastern Blue-Tongued Skink

Skink

Scincidae

Description

Skinks are lizards belonging to the family Scincidae, a family in the infraorder Scincomorpha. With more than 1,500 described species across 100 different taxonomic genera, the family Scincidae is one of the most diverse families of lizards. Skinks are found in different habitats except arctic and subarctic regions.

Skinks look like lizards, but most species of skinks have no pronounced neck and relatively small legs. Skinks' skulls are covered by substantial bony scales, usually matching up in shape and size, while overlapping. Most species of skinks have long, tapering tails they can shed if predators grab onto them. Such species generally can regenerate the lost part of a tail, though imperfectly. A lost tail can grow back within around 3-4 months. Species with stumpy tails have no special regenerative abilities.

Most skinks are medium-sized, with snout-to-vent lengths around 4.5 inches. Skinks can often hide easily in their habitat because of their protective colouring (camouflage).

Behavior/Habitat

Skinks are very specific in their habitat as some can depend on vegetation while others may depend on land and the soil. As a family, skinks are cosmopolitan; species occur in a variety of habitats worldwide, apart from polar regions.

A trait apparent in many species of skink is digging and burrowing. Many spend their time underground where they are mostly safe from predators, sometimes even digging out tunnels for easy navigation. They also use their tongues to sniff the air and track their prey. When they encounter their prey, they chase it down until they corner it or manage to land a bite and then swallow it whole. They can be voracious hunters.

Diet

Typical prey include flies, crickets, grasshoppers, beetles, and caterpillars. Various species also eat earthworms, millipedes, centipedes, snails, slugs, isopods (woodlice, etc.), moths, small lizards (including geckos), and small rodents.

Reproduction

Although most species of skinks lay eggs in clutches, some 45% of skink species have live births. Many species are ovoviviparous, the young (skinklets) developing in eggs that hatch inside the mother's reproductive tract, and emerging as live births.

If a nest is nearby, one can expect to see 10-30 lizards within the period of a month. In parts of the southern United States, nests are commonly found in houses and apartments, especially along the coast. The nest is where the skink lays its small white eggs, up to 4-8 at a time.

PET ✔

Snapping Turtle

Chelydra serpentina

Description

The common snapping turtle (Chelydra serpentina) is a species of large freshwater turtle in the family Chelydridae. Its natural range extends from southeastern Canada, southwest to the edge of the Rocky Mountains, as far east as Nova Scotia and Florida. The three species of Chelydra and the larger alligator snapping turtles (genus Macrochelys) are the only extant chelydrids, a family now restricted to the Americas. The common snapping turtle, as its name implies, is the most widespread.

The common snapping turtle is noted for its combative disposition when out of the water with its powerful beak-like jaws, and highly mobile head and neck (hence the specific epithet serpentina, meaning "snake-like"). In water, it is likely to flee and hide underwater in sediment. The common snapping turtle has a life-history strategy characterized by high and variable mortality of embryos and hatchlings, delayed sexual maturity, extended adult longevity, and iteroparity (repeated reproductive events) with low reproductive success per reproductive event.

Females, and presumably also males, in more northern populations mature later (at 15–20 years) and at a larger size than in more southern populations (about 12 years). Lifespan in the wild is poorly known, but long-term mark-recapture data from Algonquin Park in Ontario, Canada, suggest a maximum age over 100 years.

Habitat

Common habitats are shallow ponds or streams. Some may inhabit brackish environments, such as estuaries. These sources of water tend to have an abundance of aquatic vegetation due to the shallow pools. Common snapping turtles sometimes bask—though rarely observed—by floating on the surface with only their carapaces exposed, though in the northern parts of their range, they also readily bask on fallen logs in early spring. In shallow waters, common snapping turtles may lie beneath a muddy bottom with only their heads exposed.

Diet

Snapping turtles consume both plant and animal matter, and are important aquatic scavengers, but they are also active hunters that prey on anything they can swallow, including many invertebrates, fish, frogs, reptiles (including snakes and smaller turtles), unwary birds, and small mammals.

Reproduction

This species mates from April through November. The female can hold sperm for several seasons, using it as necessary. Females travel over land to find sandy soil in which to lay their eggs. After digging a hole, the female typically deposits 25 to 80 eggs each year, guiding them into the nest with her hind feet and covering them.

PET X

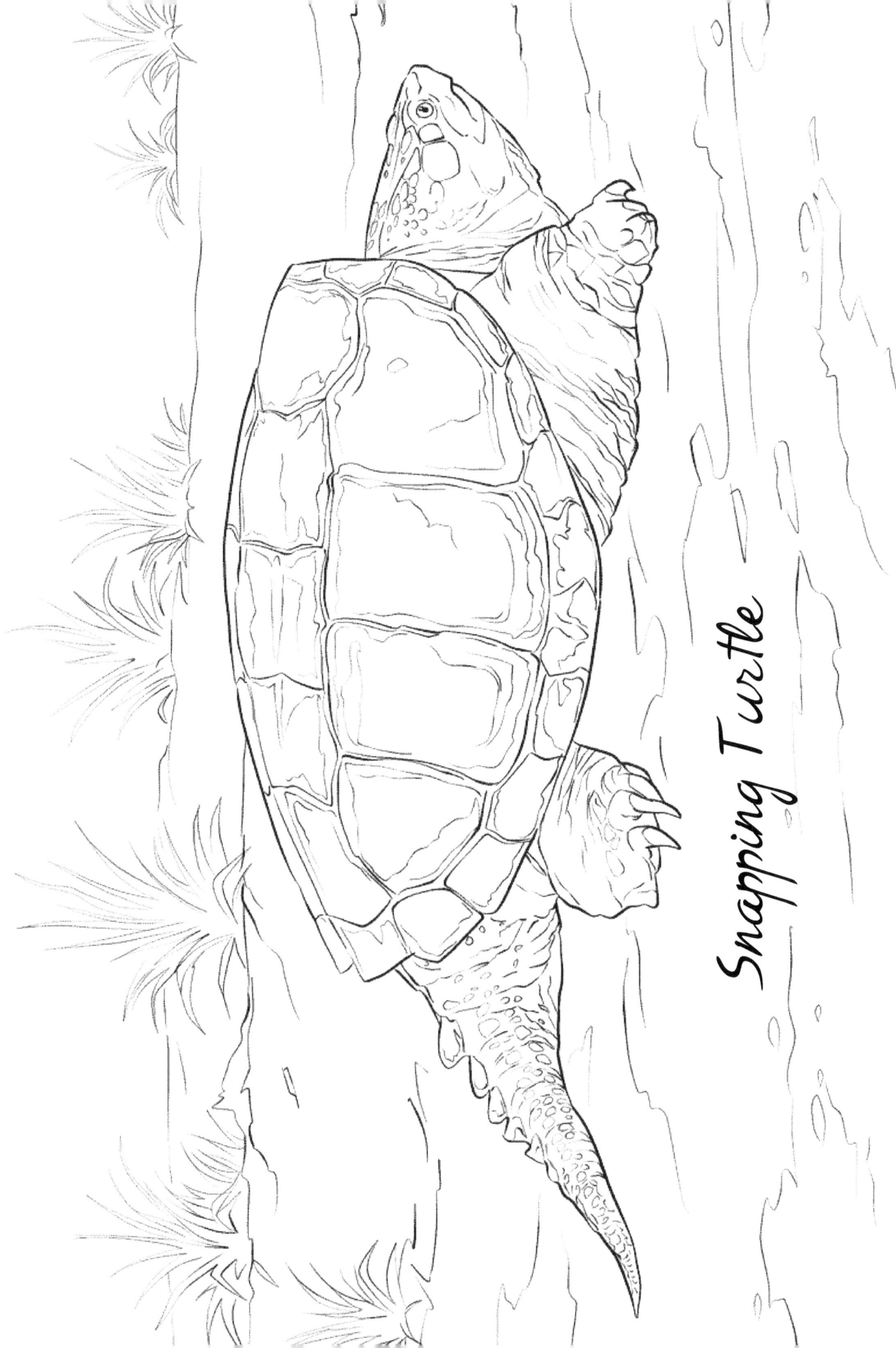

Snapping Turtle

Texas Horned Lizard

Texas Horned Lizard

Phrynosoma cornutum

Description

The Texas horned lizard is one of about 14 North American species of spikey-bodied reptiles called horned lizards, all belonging to the genus Phrynosoma. P. cornutum ranges from Colorado and Kansas to northern Mexico (in the Sonoran desert), and from southeastern Arizona to Texas. Also, isolated introduced populations are found in the Carolinas, Georgia, and Florida. Most records of the Texas horned lizard from the Piney Woods region of east Texas, Louisiana, and Arkansas are from the early and mid-twentieth century, a time when horned lizard were popular pets, and are thought to represent released or escaped pets and not the species natural range. Though some populations are stable, severe population declines have occurred in many areas of Texas and Oklahoma. The Texas spiny lizard (Sceloporus olivaceus) may be confused for a Texas horned lizard due to its appearance and overlapping habitat.

The horned lizard is popularly called a "horned toad," or "horned frog," but it is neither a toad nor a frog. The popular names come from the lizard's rounded body and blunt snout, which give it a decidedly batrachian appearance. Phrynosoma literally means "toad-bodied" and cornutum means "horned." The lizard's horns are extensions of its cranium and contain true bone.

Region/Habitat

Despite the fierce appearance, Texas horned lizards are extremely docile creatures. The Texas horned lizard is a sunbather, and requires bright sunlight to produce vitamin D. Deprived of sunlight, the animal is unable to produce vitamin D and can suffer from vitamin deficiency. They are most often found along the side of roads or other open, rocky areas, where they can lounge and take in sunlight. At night, the lizard buries itself in sand. Horned lizards are also excellent diggers, and can quickly burrow underground to escape threats.

Diet

About 70% of the Texas horned lizard's diet is made up of harvester ants, though they supplement these with termites, beetles, and grasshoppers. Texas horned lizards possess a blood plasma factor that neutralizes harvester ant venom and are known to produce copious amounts of mucus in the esophagus and pharynx which function to embed and incapacitate swallowed ants.

Reproduction

In Texas, the creature has been declared threatened and a breeding and reintroduction program has been started by the Fort Worth Zoo. Hatchlings are bred and released in targeted areas in the hope that with a large number of animals, enough will survive to grow the population in the wild. Typically in such reptile reintroduction programs, fewer than one percent of a female's offspring will survive in the wild to adulthood.

PET ✅

Tuatara

Sphenodon punctatus

Description

Tuatara (Sphenodon punctatus) are reptiles endemic to New Zealand. The name tuatara is derived from the Maori language and means "peaks on the back." Tuatara are greenish brown and grey, and measure up to 31 inches from head to tail-tip and weigh up to 2.9 pounds with a spiny crest along the back, especially pronounced in males. They have two rows of teeth in the upper jaw overlapping one row on the lower jaw, which is unique among living species. They are able to hear, although no external ear is present.

Tuatara are sometimes referred to as "living fossils." The species has between five and six billion base pairs of DNA sequence, nearly twice that of humans.

Tuatara probably have the slowest growth rates of any reptile, continuing to grow larger for the first 35 years of their lives. The average lifespan is about 60 years, but they can live to be well over 100 years old; tuatara could be the reptile with the second longest lifespan after tortoises. Some experts believe that captive tuatara could live as long as 200 years. This may be related to genes that offer protection against reactive oxygen species.

Tuatara were extinct on the mainland, with the remaining populations confined to 32 offshore islands until the first North Island release into the heavily fenced and monitored Karori Wildlife Sanctuary (now named "Zealandia") in 2005.

Region/Habitat

Adult tuatara are terrestrial and nocturnal reptiles, though they will often bask in the sun to warm their bodies. Hatchlings hide under logs and stones, and are diurnal, likely because adults are cannibalistic. Juveniles are typically active at night, but can be found active during the day.

Tuatara thrive in temperatures much lower than those tolerated by most reptiles, and hibernate during winter.

Diet

Burrowing seabirds such as petrels, prions, and shearwaters share the tuatara's island habitat during the birds' nesting seasons. The tuatara use the birds' burrows for shelter when available, or dig their own. The seabirds' guano helps to maintain invertebrate populations on which tuatara predominantly prey; including beetles, crickets, and spiders. Their diets also consist of frogs, lizards, and bird's eggs and chicks. The diet of the tuatara varies seasonally and they mainly only consume fairy prions and their eggs in the summer.

Reproduction

It takes the females between one and three years to provide eggs with yolk, and up to seven months to form the shell. It then takes 12-15 months from copulation to hatching. This means reproduction occurs at 2-5 year intervals, the slowest in any reptile. Wild tuatara are known to be still reproducing at about 60 years of age; "Henry", a male tuatara in Invercargill, New Zealand, became a father on 23 January 2009, at age 111, with an 80 year-old female.

PET ✗

Tuatara

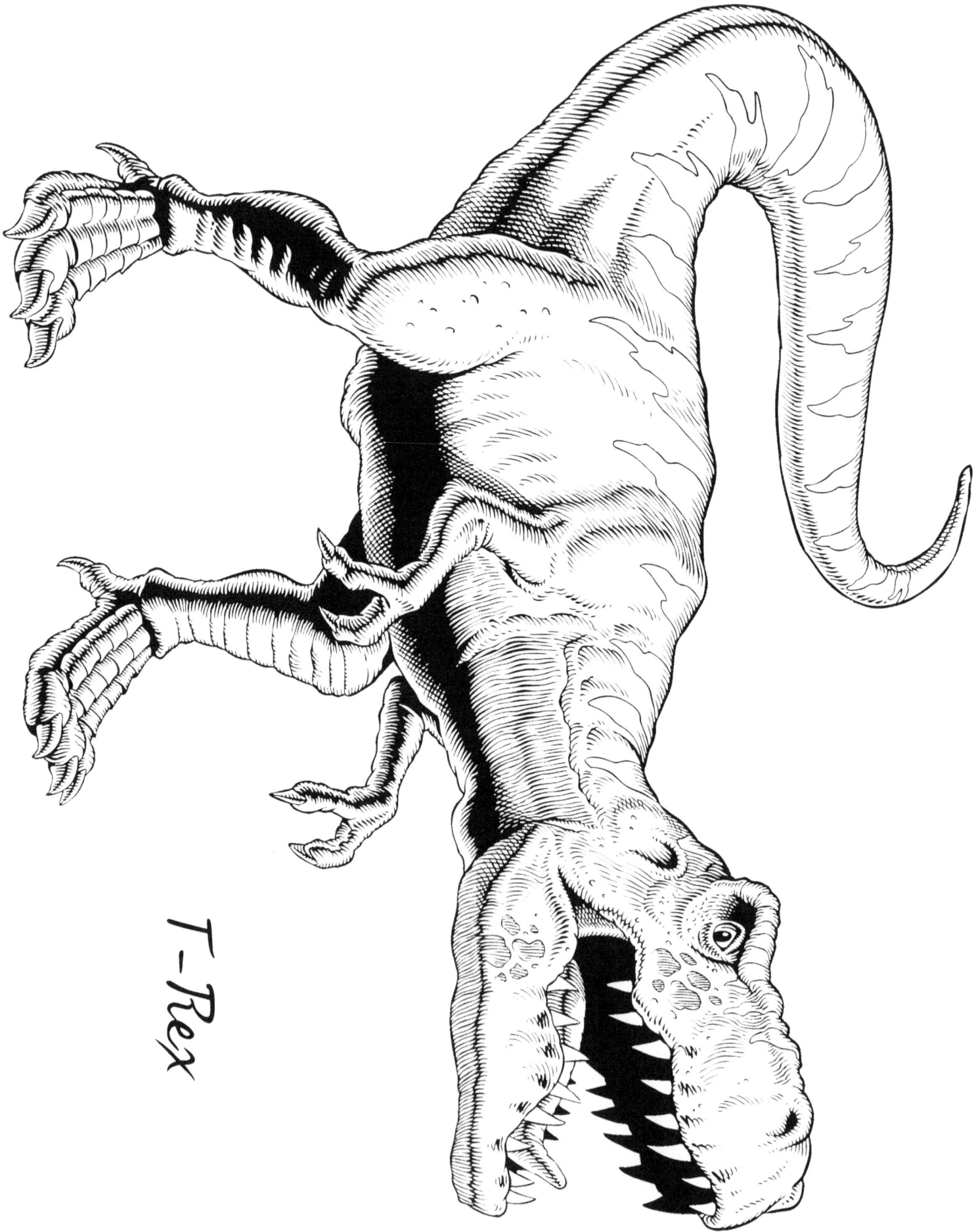

T-Rex

T-Rex

Tyrannosaurus rex

Tyrannosaurus is a genus of large theropod dinosaur. The species Tyrannosaurus rex (rex meaning "king" in Latin), often called T. rex or colloquially T-Rex, is one of the best represented theropods. Tyrannosaurus lived throughout what is now western North America. Tyrannosaurus had a much wider range than other tyrannosaurids. Fossils are found in a variety of rock formations. It was the last known member of the tyrannosaurids and among the last non-avian dinosaurs.

Like other tyrannosaurids, Tyrannosaurus was a bipedal carnivore with a massive skull balanced by a long, heavy tail. Relative to its large and powerful hind limbs, the forelimbs of Tyrannosaurus were short but unusually powerful for their size, and they had two clawed digits. T. rex could grow to lengths of over 40.7 feet, up to 12–13 feet tall at the hips, and according to most modern estimates 8.4–14 metric tons (18,500–30,800 pounds) in weight.

Specimens of Tyrannosaurus rex include some that are nearly complete skeletons. Soft tissue and proteins have been reported in at least one of these specimens. The abundance of fossil material has allowed significant research into many aspects of its biology, including its life history and biomechanics. The feeding habits, physiology, and potential speed of Tyrannosaurus rex are a few subjects of debate.

Like many bipedal dinosaurs, T. rex was historically depicted as a 'living tripod,' with the body at 45 degrees or less from the vertical and the tail dragging along the ground, similar to a kangaroo. This concept dates from Joseph Leidy's 1865 reconstruction of Hadrosaurus. In 1915, convinced that the creature stood upright, the American Museum of Natural History further reinforced the notion in unveiling the first complete T. rex skeleton arranged this way. It stood in an upright pose for 77 years, until it was dismantled in 1992.

By 1970, scientists realized this pose was incorrect and could not have been maintained by a living animal, as it would have resulted in the dislocation or weakening of several joints, including the hips. The inaccurate AMNH mount inspired similar depictions in many films and paintings until the 1990s, when films such as Jurassic Park introduced a more accurate posture to the general public. Modern representations in museums, art, and film show T. rex with its body approximately parallel to the ground with the tail extended behind the body to balance the head.

Velociraptor

Velociraptor mongoliensis

Velociraptor (meaning "swift seizer" in Latin) is a genus of dromaeosaurid theropod dinosaur. Two species are currently recognized, although others have been assigned in the past. The type species is V. mongoliensis; fossils of this species have been discovered in Mongolia. A second species, V. osmolskae, was named in 2008 for skull material from Inner Mongolia, China.

It was a bipedal carnivore with a long tail and an enlarged sickle-shaped claw on each hindfoot, which is thought to have been used to tackle and tear into prey. Velociraptor can be distinguished from other dromaeosaurids by its long and low skull, with an upturned snout.

Velociraptor (commonly shortened to "raptor") is one of the dinosaur genera most familiar to the general public due to its prominent role in the Jurassic Park motion picture series. In real life, however, Velociraptor was roughly the size of a turkey, considerably smaller than the approximately 6.5 foot tall and 180 pound reptiles seen in the films (which were based on members of the related genus Deinonychus). Today, Velociraptor is well known to paleontologists, with over a dozen described fossil skeletons, the most of any dromaeosaurid. One particularly famous specimen preserves a Velociraptor locked in combat with a Protoceratops.

The "Fighting Dinosaurs" specimen, found in 1971, preserves a Velociraptor mongoliensis and Protoceratops andrewsi in combat and provides direct evidence of predatory behavior. As the animals were preserved in ancient sand dune deposits, it is thought that the animals were buried in sand, either from a collapsing dune or in a sandstorm. Burial must have been extremely fast, judging from the lifelike poses in which the animals were preserved.

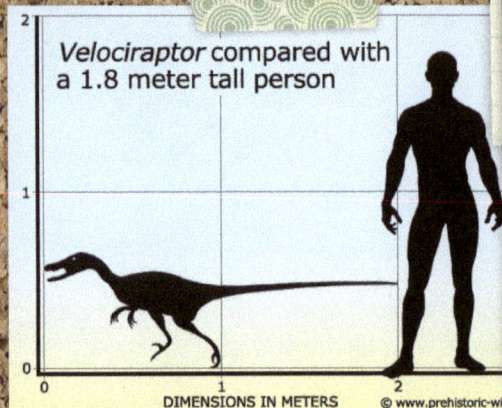

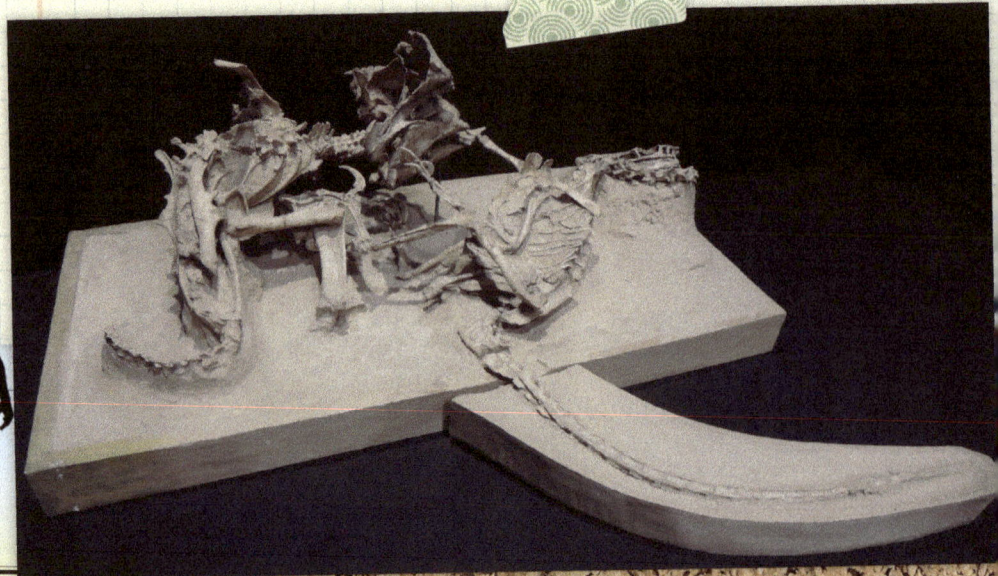

Velociraptor compared with a 1.8 meter tall person

DIMENSIONS IN METERS
© www.prehistoric-wildlife.com

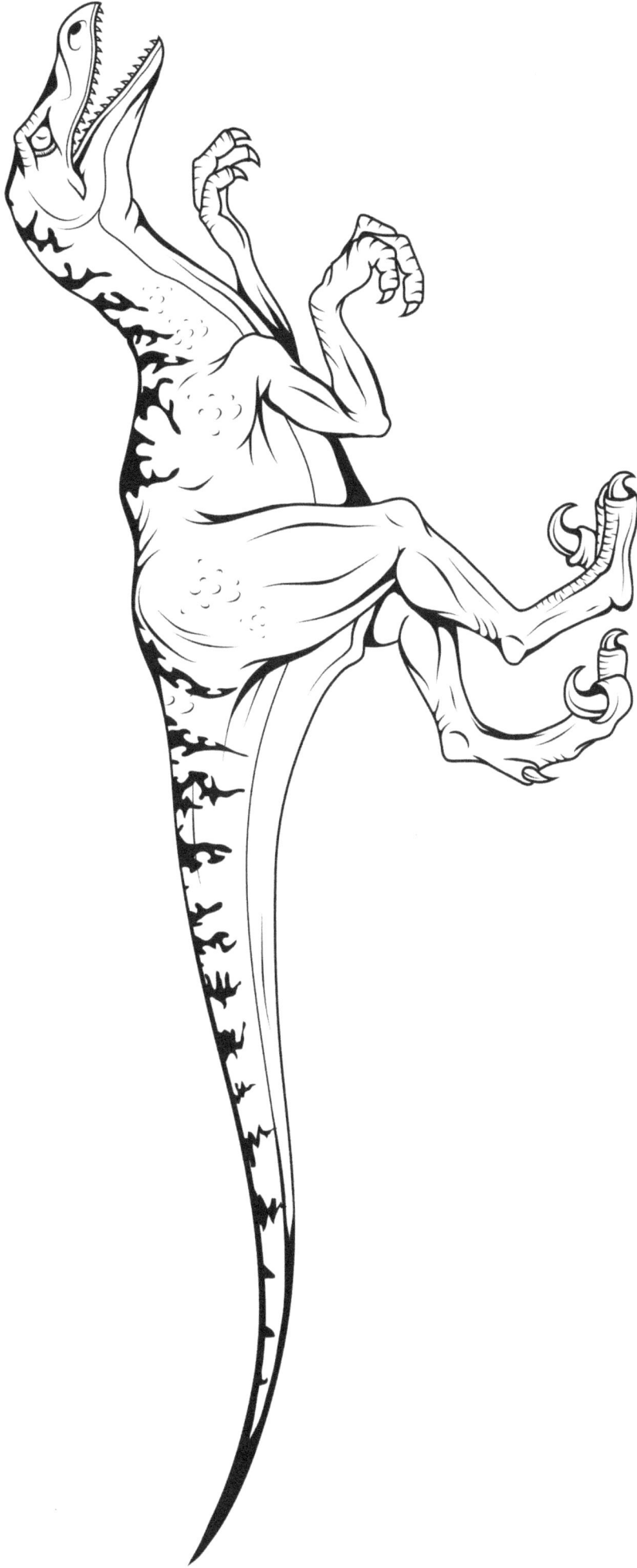

Velociraptor

Eyelash Viper

Viper

Viperidae

Description

The name "viper" is derived from the Latin word vipera, possibly from vivus ("living") and parere ("to beget"), referring to the trait viviparity (giving live birth) common in vipers, but not in snakes at large.

All viperids have a pair of relatively long hollow fangs that are used to inject venom from glands located towards the rear of the upper jaws, just behind the eyes. Each of the two fangs is at the front of the mouth on a short maxillary bone that can rotate back and forth. When not in use, the fangs fold back against the roof of the mouth and are enclosed in a membranous sheath. This rotating mechanism allows for very long fangs to be contained in a relatively small mouth. The left and right fangs can be rotated together or independently. During a strike, the mouth can open nearly 180° and the maxilla rotates forward, erecting the fangs as late as possible so that the fangs do not become damaged, as they are brittle. The jaws close upon impact and the muscular sheaths encapsulating the venom glands contract, injecting the venom as the fangs penetrate the target. This action is very fast; in defensive strikes, it will be more a stab than a bite. Viperids use this mechanism primarily for immobilization and digestion of prey. Pre-digestion occurs as the venom contains proteases, which degrade tissues. Secondarily, it is used for self defense, though in cases with nonprey, such as humans, they may give a dry bite (not inject any venom). A dry bite allows the snake to conserve its precious reserve of venom, because once it has been depleted, time is needed to replenish it, leaving the snake vulnerable. In addition to being able to deliver dry bites, vipers can inject larger quantities of venom into larger prey targets, and smaller amounts into small prey. This causes the ideal amount of predigestion for the lowest amount of venom.

Behavior/Habitat

Viperid snakes are found in the Americas, Africa, Eurasia, and South Asia. In the Americas, they are native from south of 48°N. In the Old World, viperids are located everywhere except Siberia, Ireland, and north of the Arctic Circle in Norway and Sweden. Wild viperids are not found in Australia. The adder, a viperid, is the only venomous snake found in Great Britain.

Hemotoxic venom takes more time than neurotoxic venom to immobilize prey, so viperid snakes need to track down prey animals after they have been bitten, in a process known as "prey relocalization." Vipers are able to do this via certain proteins contained in their venom.

Diet

Adults generally feed on small mammals and birds, while juveniles predominantly eat lizards. Larger prey are struck, released, tracked, and swallowed, while smaller prey is swallowed without using the venom apparatus.

PET ✕

Reproduction

Most are ovoviviparous: the eggs are retained inside the mother's body, and the young emerge living. However, a few lay eggs in nests. Typically, the number of young in a clutch remains constant, but as the weight of the mother increases, larger eggs are produced, yielding larger young.

Be sure to leave us a review on Amazon and enjoy other books by

Current and upcoming titles:

Learn and Color Nature Series

Medicinal Herbs

Freshwater Fish

Garden Plants

Trees

Bugs and Insects

Fossils

Learn and Color Stained Glass Series

Landscapes & Seascapes

Fish & Fowl

Flowers

Learn and Color Historical Figures Series

Early Civilization

The Ancient World

The Middle Ages

The Renaissance and Reformation

The Industrial Revolution

The Modern Age

The Computer Age